The Kiss

First published in Great Britain in 1996 by
BROCKHAMPTON PRESS
20 Bloomsbury Street, London WC1B 3QA
a member of the Hodder Headline Group

This series of little gift books was made by Frances Banfield, Andrea P.A. Belloli, Polly Boyd,
Kate Brown, Stefano Carantino, Laurel Clark, Penny Clarke, Clive Collins, Jack Cooper, Melanie Cumming,
Nick Diggory, John Dunne, Deborah Gill, David Goodman, Paul Gregory, Douglas Hall, Lucinda Hawksley,
Maureen Hill, Dennis Hovell, Dicky Howett, Nick Hutchison, Douglas Ingram, Helen Johnson, C.M. Lee,
Simon London, Irene Lyford, John Maxwell, Patrick McCreeth, Morse Modaberi, Tara Neill, Sonya Newland,
Anne Newman, Grant Oliver, Ian Powling, Terry Price, Michelle Rogers, Mike Seabrook,
Nigel Soper, Karen Sullivan and Nick Wells.

Compilation and selection copyright © 1996 Brockhampton Press.

ISBN 1 86019 4729
A copy of the CIP data is available from the British Library upon request.

Produced for Brockhampton Press by Flame Tree Publishing,
a part of The Foundry Creative Media Company Limited,
The Long House, Antrobus Road, Chiswick W4 5HY.

Printed and bound in Italy by L.E.G.O. Spa.

C E L E B R A T I O N

The Kiss

Selected by Karen Sullivan

BROCKHAMPTON PRESS

When we two parted
In silence and tears,
Half broken-hearted,
To sever for years,
Pale grew thy cheek and cold,
Colder thy kiss;
Truly that hour foretold
Sorrow to this!

Lord Byron, *'When We Two Parted'*

But farewell for now, my little one, my darling. Do you think of me too somctimes, but nice, sweet thoughts? So you're coming on Sunday now, right, sweetheart? I've already saved up so many kisses that if the bowl overflows they'll all be gone. So for now, tender kisses and best wishes…

Mileva Maric to Albert Einstein

God bless you! Sterne says that is equal to a kiss – yet I would rather give you the kiss into the bargain, glowing with gratitude to Heaven, and affection to you. I like the word affection, because it signifies something habitual; and we are soon to meet, to try whether we have mind enough to keep our hearts warm.

Mary Wollstonecraft to Gilbert Imlay

She said, maids must kiss no men,
Till they did for good and all.

Nicholas Breton, *The Ploughman's Song*

See the mountains kiss high heaven
And the waves clasp one another;
No sister-flower would be forgiven
If it disdain'd its brother:
And the sunlight clasps the earth,
And the moonbeams kiss the sea –
What are all these kissings worth,
If thou kiss me not.

Percy Bysshe Shelley, *'Love's Philosophy'*

Love is kisses.

Luke, 2

And thus betrayed,
Or that I wist
Farewell, unkissed!

Sir Thomas Wyatt, *'Farewell'*

You can't see a kiss.

Cole, 5

Mum likes hugs
And Mum likes kisses.
And most of all
Likes help with dishes!

American proverb

What lips my lips have kissed, and where, and why,
I have forgotten, and what arms have lain
Under my head till morning...

Edna St Vincent Millay, *'Sonnet'*

When gorse is not in bloom, kissing's out of season.

Anonymous

Why every one as they like;
as the good woman said when she kissed her cow.

Jonathan Swift

I am dying, Egypt, dying; only
I here importune death awhile, until
Of many thousand kisses the poor last
I lay upon thy lips.

William Shakespeare, *Antony and Cleopatra*

But his kiss was so sweet, and so closely he pressed,
That I languished and pined till I granted the rest.

John Gay

Stephen's kiss was lost in jest,
  Robin's lost in play,
But the kiss in Colin's eyes
  Haunts me night and day.

Sara Teasdale

The social kiss is an exchange of insincerity
between two combatants on the field of
social advancement. It places hygiene before
affection and condescension before all else.

Sunday Correspondent

When women kiss it always reminds one of
prize-fighters shaking hands.

H. L. Mencken

Drink to me only with thine eyes,
And I will pledge with mine;
Or leave a kiss but in the cup,
And I'll not look for wine.

Ben Jonson, *'To Celia'*

What is love? 'Tis not hereafter;
Present mirth hath present laughter;
What's to come is still unsure;
In delay there lies no plenty;
Then come kiss me, sweet and twenty,
Youth's a stuff will not endure.

William Shakespeare, *Twelfth Night*

Kisses honeyed by oblivion.

George Eliot

Gin a body meet a body
Coming through the rye;
Gin a body kiss a body,
Need a body cry?

Robert Burns, *'Coming Through the Rye'*

'To confess, then,' murmured Izz, 'I made sure today that he was going to kiss me as he held me; and I lay still against his breast, hoping and hoping, and never moved at all. But he did not. I don't like biding here at Talbothay's any longer! I shall go home.'

The air of the sleeping-chamber seemed to palpitate with the hopeless passion of the girls. They writhed feverishly under the oppressiveness of an emotion thrust on them by cruel Nature's law – an emotion which they had neither expected nor desired. The incident of the day had fanned the flame that was burning the inside of their hearts out, and the torture was almost more than they could endure. The differences which distinguished them as individuals were abstracted by this passion, and each was but a portion of one organism called sex.

Thomas Hardy, *Tess of the D'Urbervilles*

You teach me how cruel you've been – cruel and false. Why did you despise me? Why did you betray your own heart, Cathy? I have not one word of comfort. You may deserve this. You have killed yourself. Yes, you may kiss me, and cry, and wring out my kisses and tears; they'll blight you – they'll damn you. You loved me; then what right had you to leave me. What right – answer me – for the poor fancy you felt for Linton? Because misery, and degradation, and death, and nothing that God or Satan could inflict would have parted us, you of your own free will, did it.

Emily Brontë, *Wuthering Heights*

Sweet Helen! Make me immortal with a kiss!

Christopher Marlowe, *Faustus*

Oh fie, Miss, you must not kiss and tell.

William Congreve, *Love for Love*

Well dear we went into the front room alone and he kissed me, opened
my dress and kissed my breasts too, and he said how he felt I was his.
He was just going away when he came back and pleaded with me
dear to give him everything a woman can give a man. I told him I was
sure we should regret it but no dear anything that would make me his.
Well dear, I did! The tears I have shed have quite washed away any
wrong I did.

Minna Simmons to Ruth Slate, 1916

Oh, a kiss! Long as my exile!

William Shakespeare, *Coriolanus*

Kiss me times a thousand o'er.

Catullus, *Carmina*

But had a wist, before I kist,
That love had been sae ill to win,
I had lock'd my heart in a case o' gowd,
And pinn'd it wi' a siller pin.

Traditional ballad

 28

Never let a fool kiss you, or a kiss fool you.

Joey Adams

Kissing your hand may make you feel very good,
but a diamond bracelet lasts forever.

Anita Loos

There used to be two kinds of kisses. First when girls were kissed and deserted; second, when they were engaged. Now there's a third kind, where the man is kissed and deserted. If Mr. Jones of the nineties bragged he'd kissed a girl, everyone knew he was through with her. If Mr. Jones of 1919 brags the same everyone knows it's because he can't kiss her any more. Given a decent start any girl can beat a man nowadays.

F. Scott Fitzgerald

What did that mean, to kiss? You put your face up like that to say goodnight and then his mother put her face down. That was to kiss. His mother put her lips on his cheek; her lips were soft and they wetted his cheek; and they made a tiny little noise: kiss. Why did people do that with their two faces?

James Joyce

He speaks it as if the words were in capitals and most often he says it to the cloud of her hair beneath his chin.

He lays his hand flat against the side of her face and with his long, slim fingers touches gently the skin around her eyes. He says they must always be honest with each other and he kisses her on the lips which has the habit of making her head spin with tenderness but also sometimes with confusion so that she lays her head back upon his shoulder to calm herself and also to consider how she can feel this cherished and also this cheated.

Carol Clewlow, *A Woman's Guide to Adultery*

'Just kiss me.'... 'Where do the noses go?
I always wondered where the noses go.'
'Look, turn thy head' and then their mouths
were tight together.

Ernest Hemingway, *For Whom the Bell Tolls*

 33

I dare not ask a kiss;
I dare not beg a smile;
Lest having that, or this,
I might grow proud the while.

Robert Herrick, *'To Electra'*

A kiss may ruin a human life.

Oscar Wilde

Kiss till the cow comes home.

Francis Beaumont and John Fletcher, *Scornful Lady*

Oh what lies there are in kisses!

Heinrich Heine

Nobody wants to kiss when they are hungry.

Dorothy Dix

There's a chick and a dude in a little canoe
And the moon is shining all around
When he dipped in his paddle, it hardly even made a sound.
Well, they talked and they talked till the moon went in
And he said you better kiss me or get out and swim
So you know what to do in a little canoe
When the moon is shining all-a
The moon is shining all-a
The moon is shining all around
Get out and swim?
What the heck!
Stay and neck!
For an hour or two, or three, or four, or more.

American campfire song

 38

Idylle: From the French of Vauquelin de Fresnaye,
1536—1606

Idylle

Between red roses and white lilies
Sweetly slept my tender Phyllis,
Whilst, engaged in leap and chase,
Around her played in frolic rare
The little loves, who from the air
Desired to see her lovely face.

Enraptured, there I stood to gaze
On beauty far beyond all praise.
Then my soul did say to me :
" Fool, why tarry ? Time once lost
In more than gold accounts a cost,
And seldom may recovered be."

Then, stooping low, and on soft tread
I drew anigh, with bended head.
I touched her lips, and in that kiss
I savoured such divine delights
As taste, I think, those happy wights
Who dwell above in God his bliss.

DRAWN BY E. H. SHEPARD. TRANSLATION FROM THE FRENCH BY BARBARA BINGLEY.

My sweet little one, how I'd like to hold you and cover you
with kisses – how happy I have been with you.

Simone de Beauvoir to Jean-Paul Sartre, 1939

People who throw kisses are hopelessly lazy.

Bob Hope

Whoever named it necking was a poor judge of anatomy.

Groucho Marx

Breathless, we flung us on the windy hill,
Laughed in the sun, and kissed the lovely grass.

Rupert Brooke, *'The Hill'*

Shall we go learn to kiss, to kiss?

Nicholas Breton, *Wooing in a Dream*

I fear thy kisses, gentle maiden,
Thou needest not fear mine;
My spirit is too deeply laden
Ever to burthen thine.

Percy Bysshe Shelley, *'I Fear Thy Kisses'*

She had dislodged a stack of his cards, but he kindly refrained from straightening them and instead reached out one arm and drew her in. 'There now, sweetheart,' he said, and he settled her next to him. Still holding her close, he transferred a four of spades to a five, and Maggie rested her head against his chest and watched. He had arrived at the interesting part of the game by now, she saw. He had passed that early, superficial stage when any number of moves seemed possible, and now his choices were narrower and he had to show real skill and judgement. She felt a little stir of something that came over her like a flush, a sort of inner buoyancy, and she lifted her face to kiss the warm blade of his cheekbone. Then she slipped free and moved to her side of the bed, because tomorrow they had a long car trip to make and she knew he would need a good night's sleep before they started.

Anne Tyler, *Breathing Lessons*

You evidently have a dimple just above the corner of your mouth, stage right which is really left? When you smile at me, a little light on your cheek and you're so radiantly beautiful. I wanted to send you a little drawing to show the parts of my right-hand face that are still hyper-sensitive, perhaps always will be? So if I jump, in one of our long and lovely kissing seances you won't think it's your fault, my consummately careful darling. I wish we were in the middle of one right now, silently moving over each other's faces with resting-places, passionate ones, to linger at and in.

Mary Meigs, *To 'R'*

The moth's kiss, first!
Kiss me as if you made me believe
You were not sure, this even,
How my face, your flower, has pursed
Its petals up; so, here and there
You brush it, till I grow aware
Who wants me, and wide ope I burst.

The bee's kiss now!
Kiss me as if you enter'd gay
My heart at some noonday,
A bud that dares not disallow
The claim, so all is render'd up,
And passively its shatter'd cup
Over your head to sleep I bow.

Robert Browning, *'In a Gondola'*

We were reading one day of Lancelot in the clutches
of love. We were alone and felt no shame. Often our
eyes met across the page and we blushed; it was in
one sudden moment that we were won. When we
read that the longed-for lips were kissed by such a
lover, he, who would never then be parted from me,
tremblingly kissed my lips. Galeotto was the name
and author of the book. We read no more that day.

Dante Alighieri, *Inferno*

Let him kiss me with the kisses of his mouth.

Song of Solomon, I: 21

If you are ever in doubt as to whether or
not you should kiss a pretty girl, always
give her the benefit of the doubt.

Thomas Carlyle

And blessings on the falling out
That all the more endears,
When we fall out with those we love
And kiss again with tears!

Alfred, Lord Tennyson, *The Princess*

'...I am sure they will be married very soon, for he has got a lock of her hair.'

'Take care, Margaret. It may only be the hair of some great uncle of his.'

'But indeed, Elinor, it is Marianne's I am almost sure it is, for I saw him cut it off. Last night after tea, when you and mama went out of the room, they were whispering and talking together as fast as could be, and he seemed to be begging something of her, and presently he took up her scissors and cut off a long lock of her hair, for it was all tumbled down her back; and he kissed it, and folded it up in a piece of white paper, and put it into his pocket-book.'

Jane Austen, *Sense and Sensibility*

A legal kiss is never as good as a stolen one.

Guy de Maupassant

My little lover, here you are
Upon a big bed with mamma.
You frolic and you jig and kick
And as you dribble your morning milk
You knead my neck with hand of silk;
O young joy of the spring-tide earth,
You find me fair and full of mirth;
We love and we caress each other;
How merrily do we together
Chuckle to see the dusty light
That dances here for our delight!
I kiss and hold you and surmise
Your happy future from your eyes.

Cecile Sauvage, *My Little Lover*

But my kisses bring again, bring again
Seals of love, but seal'd in vain, seal'd in vain.

William Shakespeare, *Measure for Measure*

Stolen sweets are always sweeter,
Stolen kisses much completer,
Stolen looks are nice in chapels,
Stolen, stolen, be your apples.

James Henry Leigh Hunt, *Song of Fairies Robbing an Orchard*

Jenny kissed me when we met,
Jumping from the chair she sat in;...
Say I'm growing old, but add,
Jenny kissed me.

James Henry Leigh Hunt, *Rondeau*

She took me to her elfin grot,
And there she wept and sighed full sore,
And there I shut her wild, wild eyes
With kisses four.

John Keats, *'La Belle Dame Sans Merci'*

Kissed her once by the pigsty when she wasn't looking and never kissed her again although she was looking all the time.

Dylan Thomas, *Under Milk Wood*

Since there's no help, come let us kiss and part.

Michael Drayton, *'Since There's No Help'*

For when two friends meet
during the Easter holy days,
they come and take one
another by the hand; then
one of them saith, 'The
Lord, or Christ, is risen',
the other answereth, 'It is
so of a truth', and then they
kiss and exchange their
eggs, both men and women,
continuing in kissing
4 days together.

*Return of the first Muscovite
Ambassador, with a description
of Russia, 1558*

Give me a thousand kisses, then a hundred,
then another thousand, then a second hundred,
then yet another thousand, then a hundred.

Catullus

Wine and cakes for gentlemen,
Hay and corn for horses,
A cup of ale for good old wives,
And kisses for young lasses.

Traditional

I stole a kiss of great sweetness
Which done was out avisedness.

Charles of Orleans, *A Lover's Confession*

A kiss is what you do to your dolls and your
mother. And your father if he's home from work.

Lucy, 4

My lips two blushing pilgrims ready stand
To smooth that rough touch with a tender kiss.

William Shakespeare, *Romeo and Juliet*

We sit and talk, and kiss away the hours
As chastely as the morning dews kiss flowers.

Thomas Randolph, *'An Elegie'*

You crave one kiss of my clay-cold lips;
But my breath smells earthy strong;
If you have one kiss of my clay-cold lips,
Your time will not be long.

Anonymous, *The Unquiet Grave*

Love, which had been long deluded,
Was with kisses sweet concluded.

Nicholas Breton, *The Ploughman's Song*

My love-longing, and I can hardly miss
Some favour from her, at the least a kiss.

Geoffrey Chaucer, *'The Miller's Tale'*

Fairer than younger beauties, more beloved
Than many a wife,
By stress of Time's vicissitudes unmoved
From settled calm of life;

Endearing rectitude to those who watch
The verdict of your face,
Raising and making gracious those who catch
A semblance of your grace:

With kindly lips of welcome, and with pleased Propitious eyes benign,
Accept a kiss of homage from your least
Last Valentine.

Christina Rossetti, Valentines to My Mother

No man can print a kiss; lines may deceive.

Fluke Greville, Lord Brooke, *Myra*

Being kissed by a man who didn't wax his moustache was
– like eating an egg without salt.

Rudyard Kipling, *The Story of the Gadsbys*

I wasn't kissing her, I was just whispering in her mouth.

Chico Marx, *Marx Brothers Scrapbook*

I am in favour of preserving the French habit of kissing
ladies' hands – after all, one must start somewhere.

Sacha Guitry

Make me immortal with a kiss!
Her lips suck forth my soul.

Christopher Marlowe, *Faustus*

A kiss is a lovely trick
designed by nature to stop
speech when words become
superfluous.

Ingrid Bergman

One of those quick, awkward kisses
where each of you gets a nose in the eye.

Clive James, *Unreliable Memoirs*

O love! O fire! once he drew
With one long kiss my whole soul thro'
My lips, as sunlight drinketh dew.

Alfred, Lord Tennyson, *'Fatima'*

Georgie Porgie, pudding and pie,
Kissed the girls and made them cry;
When the boys came out to play
Georgie Porgie ran away.

English nursery rhyme

About a question of marriage I have seen
women who hate each other kiss and cry
together quite fondly. How much more do
they feel when they love!

William Makepeace Thackeray, *Vanity Fair*

Lolita, light of my life, fire of my loins. My sin,
my soul. Lo-lee-ta: the tip of the tongue
taking a trip of three steps down the palate to
tap, at three, on the teeth. Lo. Lee. Ta.

Vladimir Nabokov, *Lolita*

Few men know how to kiss well; fortunately,
I've always had time to teach them.

Mae West

'I saw you take his kiss!' 'Tis true.'
'O modesty!' 'Twas strictly kept:
He thought me asleep; at least, I knew
He thought I thought he thought I slept.'

Coventry Patmore, *The Angel in the House*

Yet each man kills the thing he loves,
By each let this be heard,
Some do it with a bitter look,
Some with a flattering word,
The coward does it with a kiss,
The brave man with a sword.

Oscar Wilde, *'The Ballad of Reading Gaol'*

When she comes home again! A thousand ways
I fashion, to myself, the tenderness
Of my glad welcome: I shall tremble – yes;
And touch her as when first in the old days
I touched her girlish hand, nor dared upraise
Mine eyes, such was my faint heart's sweet distress.
Then silence: And the perfume of her dress:
The room will sway a little, and a haze
Cloy eyesight – soul-sight, even – for a space:
And tears – yes; and the ache here in the throat,
To know that I so ill-deserve the place
Her arms make for me; and the sobbing note
I stay with kisses, ere the tearful face
Again is hidden in the old embrace.

James Whitcomb Riley, *When She Comes Home*

My kisses are his daily feast.

Thomas Lodge, *Rosalind's Madrigal*

In holiday gown, and my new-fangled hat,
Last Monday I tripped to the fair;
I held up my head, and I'll tell you for what,
Brisk Roger I guessed would be there:
He woos me to marry whenever we meet,
There's honey sure dwells on his tongue!
He hugs me so close, and he kisses so sweet,
I'd wed – if I were not too young.

John Cunningham, *Holiday Gown*

What of soul was left, I wonder, when the kissing had to stop.

Robert Browning, *A Toccata of Galuppi's*

The sound of a kiss is not so loud as that of a cannon, but its echo
lasts a great deal longer.

Oliver Wendell Holmes Sr, *The Professor at the Breakfast Table*

A kiss can be a comma, a question mark or an exclamation point.
That's basic spelling that every woman ought to know.

Mistinguett

I kissed my first girl and smoked my first cigarette on the same day.
I haven't had time for tobacco since.

Arturo Toscanini

Kissing is a means of getting two people so close together
that they can't see anything wrong with each other.

Rene Yasenek

Won't you let me kiss you goodnight? Is it something I said?

Tom Ryan

A kiss is but a kiss now! and no wave
Of a great flood that whirls me to the sea.
But, as you will! we'll sit contentedly,
And eat our pot of honey on the grave.

George Meredith

I remember – I remember well –
The first girl that I kissed.
She closed her eyes, I closed mine,
And then – worst luck – we missed!

Anonymous

A kiss, when all is said, what is it?
An oath that's given closer than before;
A promise more precise; the sealing of
Confessions that till then were barely breathed;
A rosy dot placed on the i in loving;
A secret that's confided to a mouth
And not to ears.

Edmond Rostand, *Cyrano de Bergerac*

O Susan, Susan, lovely dear,
My vows shall ever true remain;
Let me kiss off that falling tear;
We only part to meet again.
Change as ye list, ye winds;
   my heart shall be
The faithful compass that still
   points to thee.

John Gay, *Black-Eyed Susan*

How delicious is the winning
Of a kiss at love's beginning,
When two mutual hearts are sighing
For the knot there's no untying.

Thomas Campbell, *Freedom and Love*

...these kisses on paper are scarce worth keeping.
You gave me one on my neck that night you were
in such good humour, and one on my lips on
some forgotten occasion, that I would not part
with for a hundred thousand paper ones.

Thomas Carlyle

When her loose gown from her shoulders did fall,
And she me caught in her arms long and small,
Therewith all sweetly did me kiss
And softly said, 'Dear heart how like you this?'

Sir Thomas Wyatt, *They Flee From Me*

Notes on Illustrations

Page 1 *The Rose Bower* by H. Zatzka (Josef Mensing Gallery, Hamm-Rhynern). Courtesy of The Bridgeman Art Library; **Page 3** *Etude pour La Danse a la Campagne* by Pierre Auguste Renoir (Christie's London). Courtesy of The Bridgeman Art Library; **Page 4** *Early Summer* by Alfred Wooler (Waterhouse and Dodd, London). Courtesy of The Bridgeman Art Library; **Page 7** *Britomart and Amoret* by Mary F. Raphael (Christopher Wood Gallery). Courtesy of The Bridgeman Art Library; **Page 9** *Husking Corn* by Simon Hollosy (Magyar Nemzeti Galeria, Budapest). Courtesy of The Bridgeman Art Library; **Page 11** *Gone With The Wind.* Courtesy of the British Film Institute; **Page 12** *Sisley and Wife (The engaged couple)* by Pierre Auguste Renoir (Wallraf-Richartz Museum, Cologne). Courtesy of The Bridgeman Art Library; **Page 15** *The Kiss* by Francesco Hayez (Pinacoteca di Brera, Milan). Courtesy of The Bridgeman Art Library; **Page 17** *Mother's Kiss.* Courtesy of The Laurel Clark Collection; **Page 18** *La Belle Dame Sans Merci* by John William Waterhouse (Hessisches Landesmuseum, Darmstadt). Courtesy of The Bridgeman Art Library; **Page 21** *Reine de Joie par Victor Jose* by Henri de Toulouse-Lautrec (Private collection). Courtesy of The Bridgeman Art Library; **Page 25** *The Betrothal of Robert Burns and Highland Mary* by James Archer (Forbes Magazine Collection, London). Courtesy of The Bridgeman Art Library; **Page 26** *The Kiss* by Gustav Klimt (Osterreichische Galerie, Vienna). Courtesy of The Bridgeman Art Library; **Page 29** *The Suitor* by Madeleine Lemaire (Fine-Lines (Fine Art), Warwickshire). Courtesy of The Bridgeman Art Library; **Page 30** *Julie, or the First Kiss of Love,* engraving by Jacques Louis Copia by J. B. Mallet (Stapleton Collection). Courtesy of the Bridgeman Art Library; **Pages 34-5** *Lovers in the Kitchen* by Johann Kurtweil (Cider House Galleries, Ltd., Bletchingley). Courtesy of The Bridgeman Art Library.; **Page 37** *Autumn Lovers, Front Cover of the Pictorial Review, November 1909, Vol.11* (Private Collection). Courtesy of The Bridgeman Art Library; **Page 39** *The Rendez-vous* by Pablo Picasso (Pushkin Museum, Moscow). Courtesy of The Bridgeman Art Library; **Page 40** *Idylle: From the French of Vauquelin de Fresnaye.* Courtesy of The Laurel Clark Collection; **Page 43** *The Kiss* by G. Baldry (Simon Carter Gallery, Woodbridge). Courtesy of The Bridgeman Art Library; **Page 47** *'For one delicious moment she submitted to his caress'.* Courtesy of The Laurel Clark Collection; **Page 48** *Lovers Embracing on a Terrace,* Greeting Card, c.1900 (Private Collection). Courtesy of The Bridgeman Art Library; **Page 51** *Gathering Honey* by Harrison Fisher (Private Collection). Courtesy of The Bridgeman Art Library; **Page 53** *Mistinguett and Max Dearly Dancing the Waltz* by Rene Bertrand (Private Collection). Courtesy of The Bridgeman Art Library; **Page 55** *The Stolen Kiss* by Jean-Honore Fragonard (Hermitage, St. Petersburg). Courtesy of The Bridgeman Art Library; **Page 57** *Great Grandmamma's Love Story.* Courtesy of The Laurel Clark Collection;

Page 58 *Saying Hello to Kitty*, Victorian postcard (Private Collection). Courtesy of The Bridgeman Art Library; Page 61 *The Suitor* by Adrian Moreau (John Noott Galleries, Broadway, Worcestershire). Courtesy of The Bridgeman Art Library; Page 65 *Rinaldo and Armida* by Francesco Hayez (Museo d'Arte Moderno di ca Pesaro, Venice). Courtesy of The Bridgeman Art Library; Page 66 *Lovers in the Road* by Pablo Picasso (Musee Picasso, Barcelona). Courtesy of The Bridgeman Art Library; Page 69 *Abelard Soliciting the Hand of Helouise* by Angelica Kauffman (Burghley House, Stamford, Linconshire). Courtesy of The Bridgeman Art Library; Page 71 *Lovers by a Fountain* by Modesto Faustini (Bonhams, London). Courtesy of The Bridgeman Art Library; Page 75 *The Rest* by Francois Boucher (Noortman (London)Ltd.). Courtesy of The Bridgeman Art Library; Page 76 *Love* by Konstantin Andreyevich Somov (Armenian State Picture Gallery, Yerevan). Courtesy of The Bridgeman Art Library. Page 79 *The Milk Sop* by Thomas Rowlandson (Victoria and Albert Museum, London). Courtesy of the Bridgeman Art Library; Pages 80-1 *Teatime Romance* by Hermann Koch (Josef Mensing Gallery, Hamm-Rhynern).Courtesy of The Bridgeman Art Library; Page 83 *The Alarm* by Jean Francois de Troy (Victoria and Albert Museum). Courtesy of The Bridgeman Art Library.

Acknowledgements: The Publishers wish to thank everyone who gave permission to reproduce the quotes in this book. Every effort has been made to contact the copyright holders, but in the event that an oversight has occurred, the publishers would be delighted to rectify any omissions in future editions of this book. Sarah Teasdale from *Collected Poems 1928-1953,* published by Macmillan © 1915 renewed 1943 by Mamie T. Wheless. Reprinted with permission of Macmillan Publishing Co. Ltd; *The Divine Comedy* by Dante Alighieri, translated by John D. Sinclair, reprinted with permission from The Bodley Head; Letter of Minna Simmons from *Dear Girl: The Diaries and Letters of Two Working Women 1897–1917,* edited by Tierl Thompson, copyright © Tierl Thompson, 1987. Reprinted by permission of The Women's Press Ltd; Simone de Beauvoir, from *Letters to Sartre,* translated and edited by Quintin Haore, with an introduction by Sylvie Le Bon de Beauvoir. Published by Radius, 1991, reprinted by permission of Hutchinson Ltd; Anne Tyler, *Breathing Lessons* © Anne Tyler, published by Vintage, a division of Random House, reprinted by permission of Random House UK and New York; *Good News Study Bible,* published by Thomas Nelson, 1986, extracts reprinted with their kind permission; *Penguin Book of Japanese Verse,* translated by Geoffrey Bownas and Anthony Thwaite, published by Penguin 1964, and reprinted with their permission; James Joyce reprinted courtesy of The Bodley Head and Random House, Inc.